Inspirational Poetry and Messages from Beyond

By
Kate Newlands

BALBOA.
PRESS

A DIVISION OF HAY HOUSE

Balboa Press books may be ordered through booksellers or by contacting:

Balboa Press
A Division of Hay House
1663 Liberty Drive
Bloomington, IN 47403
www.balboapress.com.au
1-(877) 407-4847

ISBN: 978-1-4525-0178-9 (sc)
ISBN: 978-1-4525-0179-6 (e)

Library of Congress Control Number: 2011904540

Printed in the United States of America

Balboa Press rev. date: 03/19/2011

Other Books by
Kate Newlands

Journey to an Ancient Land

Acknowledgements

I would like to thank all My Guides, Spirit Family, Friends, and Angels who have helped me produce this book. Through the channelling of the poems and messages I am able to act on their behalf and give to their messages to the people of the world

I would also like to thank my family and friends on this earth plane for believing in me.

Categories Index

Who I am	1
SPIRITUAL AND INSPIRATIONAL MESSAGES	13
Spiritual Eulogy	15
Ages Past	16
Always Friends	18
Angel Guidance	19
Angel Ways	20
Archangel Michael Prayer	21
A Saying in our World	22
Beach Visit	23
Birthday Poem	24
Black Swans	25
Christmas Eve Bells	26
Cord Detached	27
Dying	28
Easter Treats	29
Excitement in the Air	30
Finalization	31
Fluttering Hearts	32
Forgiving	33
Good Friday	34
Grey Bird	35
Guardian Angels	36
Japanese lady	37
Life	38
Love Unknown	39
Moon Eclipse	40
Morning Dew	41

Night Dreams   42
Night Thoughts   43
Ocean Calling   44
Peace on Earth   45
Phone Call   46
Plane Spirits   47
Poems   48
Reality   49
Reflections of our Souls   50
Restrained Love   51
Role Reversal   52
Shedding the Past   53
Someone's Grief   54
Spirit Visit   55
Sunday Thoughts   56
The Christmas Story   58
Two Hearts   60
Unborn Child   61
Understanding   62
Wedding Message   63
Where is the Girl   64
White Light   65
Who Do They Love   66
Wondering   67
Xmas Sales   68

WAR POEMS   69

ANZAC Cove 2006   71
ANZAC Day 2008   72
ANZAC Day 2009   73
ANZAC Day 2010 from France   74
Atomic Bomb   76
Battlefields – Belgium & France 2010   77
Dedicated to John & the Crew of HMAS Sydney   78
De-Ville Wood – Longeval Cemetery 2010   79

To the Soldiers of WW1   80
Afghan War Zone   81

PAST LIFE POEMS   83

Wynnum – Brisbane   85
Angel in Disguise   86
Centuries Old Lovers   87
Chief Sitting Bull   88
Child's Dream   89
King Arthur's Mother   90
Lost Desert Children   92
Manor Days'   94
Maypole Dance   96
Loss of a Friend   98
Past War Friendship   99
Prison Camp   100
Puritans   102
Roman Army   103
Sailing Ship   104
Slave Friend   105
Smugglers   106
Titanic   107

CHANNELLED MESSAGES   109

Visitation and Channelled Message from Jesus   110
2nd Visitation and Channelled message from Jesus   112
Channelled message after Doreen Virtue's Angel
      Intuitive Seminar Australia 2010   113
Message from Arch Angel Metatron   114

EVENT POEMS   115

Aussie Outback   117
Australia Day   118
Boxing Day Tsunami   119

Camden Town   120
China Earthquake   121
Days Gone By   122
Dedicated to the Victorian Bush Fire Victims   124
Como Cinema   125
Haiti Earthquake   126
Headhunters   127
New Orleans Drowns   128
Perth Bush Fires   130
Samoan Tsunami   131
Space Flight   132
Sumatra Earthquake   133
Train Wreckage   134
Victorian Bushfires   135

EXPERIENCE POEMS   137

Britain Experiences   139
Group Outing   143
First Passenger Train to Mandurah   144
Incense Burns Out   146
Keukonhof Tulip Farm   147
Leaving Japan   148
My Ghost My Sister   149
Orbs of Spirits   150
Sleepy Town of Reefton   151
Scottish Feelings   152
Suburban Sunday Train   154
The Seal   156
The Weatherman   158
Visitors   160
Wynnum Foreshore   161
Xmas Long Ago   162

FAMOUS PEOPLE   163

Chilean Miners Rescue   165
Free Man   166
Dark Knight   168
Lasseter's Reef   169
Dedicated to Michael Jackson   170
Dedicated to Vincent Van Gogh   171

FAMILY POEMS   173

Betty   175
Bessie   176
Boy Next Door   178
Busy Bakery   179
Family Pictures   180
Jim   181
Maori Princess – Channeled From Nana   182
Man on the Hill   184
Mum   185
My American friend   186
Nan   188
New Born Child   189
Over the Air Waves   190
Poppy Brian   191
Pop   192
Sis   194
Steam Train – For Dad   195
Talented Child   196

Who I am

My spiritual journey began many years ago in the early 1970's with a lady who was a guiding light in my transition to understanding the ways of the spirit world. She has been in my life since I was a little child. But from the age of 17 when I moved to the city she lived in, she became my closest confidant in all matters and still is to this day. I call her Aunty because of the close relationship between my parents, her and her husband. Even though she is in her mid eighties and very ill she will always remain a guiding light. To this day she is still very psychic but she now asks me the questions I used to ask her. I think she has been with me in lots of lifetimes, and was in this life with me to make sure I continued on the same path, and to remind me of things we had learnt in lifetimes before.

A few years after my close association started with my aunty, I started going to see mediums and clairvoyants. As a lot of us are aware it's always inside us and we just have to develop what we know is deep in our soul. I wanted to learn it all. One lady I saw predicted that I would move countries and at that time I said I doubt that very much as

I didn't like the thought of moving from my birth country. Never giving it another thought, we moved to Australia 10 years later. I have now been here 23 years and been an Australian citizen for 10 years. I still love my birth country but I feel a really strong resonance with Australia.

I have spent a couple of past lives in this country and now understand why I was drawn to it, as well as knowing why I was in denial of coming here in the early years. I know what those lives were, and how they ended. One life was in a particular suburb in Brisbane where I love to go and visit. How I found this suburb I will explain further in this story.

My spiritual and inspirational poetry writing came into being one day six years ago when I walked into a card shop and I was looking for a sympathy card and couldn't find anything that I liked. I am not saying the cards were not good; there was just nothing that suited what I needed. As I was leaving the shop this voice in my head said "Why don't you write your own, and put it out there". I couldn't wait to write what I was being given.

On arriving home I immediately wrote my first poem. For the want of a name I called it Spiritual Eulogy. This name has stayed with it and will continue to do so. The very first reaction to the poem was "that's creepy" but I never considered it that way. It tells of how the spirit world communicates with the family and friends after they have passed over. Now everyone that reads it understands the meaning of it and likes it.

After this, poems started falling into my head from the spirit world and higher beings. I would sit and meditate and the poetry would come in, now I don't have to sit and meditate for the words, they just fall into my head. I have been able to make contact with famous people who gave me words that I turned into poem form.

I have now categorized the poems I have written – spiritual and inspirational message poems, war, past life, event, experience, famous people and family.

The war poems are given to me from the dead soldiers in WW1 & WW2, on Anzac Days, and during a recent tour of the Battlefields of France & Belgium, which was a very emotional trip. There was also another past life spent there. My feelings about this is that a lot of people who make the pilgrimage to the Battlefields of Europe had fought there in another lifetime and go back to pay their respects to their fallen mates and for closure.

When things happen around the world that causes grief or emotional feelings I am able to receive poems in relation to these events. As well as the event poems there are some about places generally, I have put these under the category of event poems. I do hope that none cause any grief to others, as this is not meant to be so, I am publishing them to share them and help people understand their own feelings.
As a Spirit Communicator I have people come through to me on a regular basis, and through talking to them I have been given interesting poems and messages. Sometimes

its very hard because you want to tell some people what you receive but are not sure how they will react, or you can't actually get in contact with them to tell them. I am often in communication with one high profile local actor who passed away not long ago; he wanted his family to know he was ok and he loved them. I know he watches down upon them all and is happy about things that are happening although he says he feels very humble.

In the past year I have been able to receive channelled messages from Jesus and Archangels, which I will also put in this book. I feel really privileged to communicate with them and look forward to many more messages. I do believe we all have angels who look after us along with our spirit families looking down and keeping an eye on us. I have had many experiences that I will share with you in a future book.

Five years ago I learnt how to do Reiki and have my Reiki 1, 2 & 3 Certificate. I felt I needed to be doing something to help people. I guess you would say the universe pushed me in the right direction and I met a lovely lady who taught me well. Reiki is a universal healing introduced into the western world by Dr Isui. Because I am only a conduit for the healing, my healers and I made a pact that I am able to receive messages from spirit for people while doing the healing. My healing guides let me know if the patient needs a healing where they are to sit or lie in the quiet totally, or if the healing is more along the physical line they will then give me messages for my clients.

As well as the Reiki I attended a local development circle for a while which was a good background for the future and helped me understand about all the feelings & senses, it also enabled me to learn how to receive messages. Meditation has a big part in clearing the mind of clutter so the ability to receive is easier. For me I can receive in or out of meditation. It took a while for me to grasp the quiet of meditation, as my mind was always very active.

Angels came into my life around 2006, I was at home in NZ and spending the day with a cousin in my families' hometown. We were going into town to look around the shops. I made a comment about not being about to get a carpark space, and my cousin was really quick to say I have asked the Angels and we will get one. Sure enough we did, in the busy main street where it looked impossible to get a parking bay. I now do this on a regular basis myself. After a discussion on angels I decided I would be looking into this more. She told me she had done the Doreen Virtue Angel Intuitive in Australia earlier in the year, and I was envious that I hadn't been able to do it. It wasn't till 2010 that the opportunity arose and I was able to attend the November 2010 Doreen Virtue AI workshop in Queensland. I had over the previous 4 years become quite close to my angels and couldn't get my hands on enough books about them amongst other subjects. I was so excited to be doing the workshop and meet some really great people there. I have found out over the years how they can help you in any way all you have to do is ask. Generally they wont step in and help unless you ask or your life is in danger. I wish to relate to you a recent story that has left a more lasting impression on me that you can imagine.

I was walking with a friend along a pathway in front of a shop recently, chatting away, I knew there were a couple of steps coming up as I had been there many times before, but I wasn't concentrating. We kept talking as we were walking along and all of a sudden I felt myself being lifted up and put down about 3 feet away. I felt like I was wrapped in someone arms and he or she had been protecting me from falling down the stairs and fracturing a bone. (Which I might add has happened a few times). My friend asked me what I was doing and I replied I don't know. By then my brain told me this was the angels saving me, I looked at where I had landed and thought that's where I could have been flat on my face. The feeling is something that I will remember for a very long time, and I felt the feeling of protection for a couple of days. All I can say is I was picked me up at the top of the steps and put back down a few feet from where I should have fallen. So thank you to my angels.

As a Spirit Communicator I have been given the ability to see, feel, hear, smell outside the normal areas of our lives. Below are five areas I have been gifted with.

Clairvoyance – where your third eye processes and gives you an image
Clairaudience – where you can hear things you wouldn't hear with your normal hearing

Clairsentience – where you feel another person's or animal's emotion or pain

Claircognizance – where you have a premonition or knowledge of something in the future

Clairalience – where you can smell something that belongs to a deceased relative or friend (This last gift I have only started being able to do recently).

I have always believed as Buddhists do that our souls evolve and we turn up again in another lifetime without memories of the previous life. Throughout our lives we come across people, places and moments that we feel comfortable with or think we know. These times and moments I personally believe we have known the same in other lifetimes.

A fine example for me was when I was visiting with friends in Brisbane in the late 1990's for the first time. Whilst travelling into the city on the train, and we were going through countryside between suburbs I was feeling a sense of knowing this area. On crossing over the rail bridge near the suburb Wynnum I felt the emotion build up inside me and felt an overwhelming knowledge inside me that I had to come back here one day. I had to return and investigate these feelings.

The next time I came to Brisbane one year later, I was visiting with different friends but they lived to far out for me to find my way to this suburb. Whilst there another couple who I knew came and picked me up to take me on a picnic. I had no idea where we were going. We drove to a place on the sea front. We decided to have this picnic at a place called the Wading Pool. Never realising the wading pool was at the same suburb that I had seen on the train the year before. While sitting and paddling out feet in the wading pool I could feel this overwhelming feeling coming over me again, and I look up and glanced around, my eyes falling upon this shop on the corner. As I stared at the shop I was taken back in time to and saw the food on the shelves and how it was laid out etc. I found out at this time that I was in Wynnum. I decided the next time I came over to Brisbane it would be devoted to checking this all out on my own.

Another 15 months past before I was able to get over. What happened was the airfares were cheap but I was unable to afford it. I asked a close friend if he would lend me the money, I would pay him back. Lucky for me he trusted me enough to do it without hesitation. I knew I had to go over there again as soon as possible.

By this time I had started doing past life meditations, had seen this suburb, and was given names of streets that I didn't even know existed at the time. These names were names of my grandmothers, and other names.

On arriving in Brisbane I chose to stay in the city, as the access to get around was really good, and I travelled by train to Wynnum the day I arrived. Upon alighting from the train I felt like I had arrived home. I wandered up the street which when I looked at the signpost was the name Edith (one of my grandmother's names). I stopped in new age shop where I made friends with the lady who owned it and when I told her my mission she was eager to give me help. I wanted to know where I could get information on the history of Wynnum.

She guided me to how to get to the Wading Pool, which I was already familiar with. Once there I sat at the pool just looking around. I went into the shop and knew I had been in before. I then started walking along the street southward. My brain didn't decide to do this; my legs and inner being just took me. It was like I was in a trance. I walked two streets, and turned right into the street I had come upon. My body stopped a couple of houses up the road and as I looked around my eyes were guided to the property I was standing outside of. I could see the house in my head that had been there, and I knew I had been definitely been here before.

I decided to go to the public library in the city and look at photos of old Wynnum, and came across some particular photos of people that I recognized immediately. Also pictures of the shops, school and wading pool as well. I went back to the Historical Society in Wynnum the next day as they had been closed the day previously, and asked to see any old photos of the town. They kindly showed me a special book that had loads of photos of old identities and scenes. There was one person whom I recognised in my mind, with the same recognition I felt at the Library. As well as names of my grandmothers being street names in Wynnum, there are people in my current life who were with me in that lifetime. There were names in the photos that are same names as friends now and in those days these names would have been extremely unusual.

Another particular instance that has a common factor after all this happened, is I was working with a lovely lady in Perth who I got along really well with. She happened to mention one day that she came from Wynnum, and as time moved on we formed a really close friendship, which I feel comes from those days. I must add she is back living close to the same suburb now and I stayed with her recently in 2010. We drove to and wandered around the suburb feeling a sense of comradery over the same place.

I wrote my first past life poem after finding out about this particular life, and I continue to visit the suburb of Wynnum each time I go to Brisbane. I also have another group of life long friends who have moved to this same suburb, and wonder if they feel the same as me but haven't acknowledged the feelings.

I have had numerous past life experiences for example Tintaginel in Cornwall England, which I have visited and felt like I had gone home. I can be drawn into photos of certain scenery and have seen a couple of era's I have lived in. One was a child in England at the time of Roman Army, and another in the early centuries as a Healer when healing was kept a secret. I have been on an Indian Reservation in USA to being a Slave in the cotton fields in USA. There are many more, which I have written poems about.

The last group of poems is dedicated to my family. Some of them relate to people who have gone back to their spirit family, and some relate to people who are still on this earth plane.

I love the wide variety of words that are given to me and enjoy writing all that is given. Now I would like to share with you a selection of messages and poems, which I have received so far.

If anyone wishes to contact me they may do so on celticangel527@gmail.com

Spiritual and Inspirational Messages

Spiritual Eulogy

Do not despair
I am here not there
I will whisper in your ear
You will know I am here

You may sense someone there
You will try to deny it
Just talk to me I'll answer
With a touch on your arm
Or a gentle breeze on your hair
Never feel fear it's only me who is there

Our souls have been entwined
Since the beginning of time
They will stay that way
Through life as you know it
Just think of me, you'll feel my love
Watching over you
Keeping you safe from above

You will feel saddened by my leaving
I have learnt life's lessons
So I go to await you
It's been a challenging path to tread
But like me you learn and overcome them
And follow me to the light at the end

Do not despair
I am here not there
I am with you in this life
And the next forever and ever

Ages Past

What do we know from ages past
Spiritual matters stay the same

People meet up in this life
Continuing work of the same

Witches were burnt at the stake
Now they've a different name

Fortunes told through crystal balls
Now Oracle cards do the same

Contacting spirit is done by some
It can help relieve others pain

Healing was through herbs all mixed
Naturopaths blend the same

Hands on healing has advanced
They call it different names

Meditation helps to relax
Those who feel stressed and strained

Breathe in and count, Breathe out and count
Your mind will never feel the same

So all out there who've come to fear
Have nothing to worry about

The people above are there to help
Just call out they hear you shout

Always Friends

Friends they'll always be
Lovers will fill their needs
Sometime in the future
They hope there'll be a sign
When they will come together
Each other will be thine

Angel Guidance

Angels are there to help you
Every step along the way
When you feel things go wrong
They are lessons to learn on the way
As you walk the path your on
Listen for guidance that comes your way
You will see when you get to the end
All the help that's been your way
Sometimes you might think its wrong
And do things your own way
But in the end the world of realms
Always guides you the right way

Angel Ways

I feel Divine Light protect me
To give me the confidence inside
To step out and do the light work
That's been planned for me this life

The angels and guides are with me
They give me messages all the time
To help pass on to the people
And be recognized at the time

My sensitivity picks up problems
From people all around
I need to learn not to take it
And make it part of my life

I surround myself in white light
Sealing it off under my feet
This divine light will protect me
From peoples feelings that run deep

Let people see I'm there to help
If they need someone around
I send them light and healing
In hope it will brighten their day

Archangel Michael Prayer

Archangel Michael
Take the pain from my heart
Take the constriction from my throat
Take the negative thoughts from my head
Take away the blockages that I feel
Take away the sadness in my heart

Give me back the passion
Give me back the joy
Give me back the feeling
Of the love I know is there
Help me feel and know the love
That's not just in my head

A Saying in our World

There is a saying in our world
That life goes round and round
It's sometimes topsy-turvy
It feels not quite right
But when you ask the spirit world
They're there to help you see
That some things in our world
Are just not meant to be
The thoughts that we have
Is a part of our wee plan
That we choose to teach us
When we come to this great land
The light I see surround us
Is showing us the way
It's there every time we ask
It's there to shine our way

Beach Visit

A picture I took with my mind
It will stay with me a long time
Whenever I wish I were there
The picture I see is very clear

Water washes over my feet
Freezing at the first touch
Cleansing me on the inside
Oh I felt the joy so much

The waves come through in layers
Four I could count from the shore
As they rolled into the land
My feet were sinking in the sand

Birthday Poem

We are reaching that age
Who would have thought
We are reaching that age
Where others been before
We are reaching that age
We think and feel the same
We are reaching that age
When we miss what's past
We are reaching that age
We still can feel the love
We are reaching that age
We see the young catch up
We are reaching that age
Where we sit back and watch
We are reaching that age
Who cares what people think
We are reaching that age
When our lives are before us
We are reaching that age
When the world is our oyster

Black Swans

Two swans on the river
Moving silently and graceful
Look out for each other
The current helps them along
The moon has been full
The stars are shining bright
Man is fishing off the jetty
His wife sitting along side
A couple sitting on the sand
Talking sweetly to the swans
They preen themselves openly
Showing off their beautiful wings

Christmas Eve Bells

The bells ring out in the night
From the church upon the hill
People gathered at the site
To pray for peace and goodwill
The celebration was the birth
Christ's life and all he achieved
Stumbling blocks along the way
Of these he paid no heed
Celebrations held every year
They will go on for many more

Cord Detached

The bond is gone
The string detached
The cord is cut
We're not attached
Now is the time
To step out there
To find the person
Who's always there
Who will let me speak
Who will believe in me
Not second best
Which is what's been

Dying

Don't be scared of death
It's another form of life
We just go to another dimension
Where we can catch our breath
We had lessons to learn this time
Else we'll be back for another round
People grieve and don't comprehend
The suffering they're meant to feel
It is part of mankind's destiny
While our feet are firmly on the ground

Easter Treats

Easters here oh what a treat
The bunnies turn up in every street
The children love it when they find
An Easter Egg oh how divine
Chocolate ends up round their mouths
All mothers do is wash them down
But who cares, its once a year
Easter Eggs always bring cheer
Hot Cross Buns taste so nice
Hot and Crispy, a sheer delight
Bakers make more than a dozen
People buy and keep them frozen

Excitement in the Air

Happy news came that day
Excitement was in the sound
The voice she heard was thick
Emotional feelings flowing
Tears started filling her eyes
He wanted to cry she knew

Gladness filled her heart
She was happy it was so
The pain hasn't finished yet
He still had lessons to grow
All she could do is be here
When his feelings flowed

Finalization

There comes a time to say goodbye to feelings you may
have
Sometimes in each other company isn't the greatest that
could be
Age comes upon some people that you don't understand
You've felt the same feelings in a life you had before
One doesn't need to have it again in the life you want to
lead
Goodbye, good luck in the future, you are free to live
your dreams

Fluttering Hearts

Hearts still flutter
For centuries gone by
They cry for each other
All through the night
They call to each other
The only way they know
One wonders for how long
They will keep up this flow
The past hasn't gone
Their hearts only know
That feelings can live forever
To the very end of time

Forgiving

The moon is rising in the sky
The stars are shining bright
Day turns gently into night
The candles shine so bright

Thoughts wonder as time goes by
What issues we left in the past
Forgiveness in the heart is needed
To get us through future lives

Good Friday

The day was still
Not a sound was heard
No chirp in the trees.
The birds were quiet
People stayed indoors
A dead sounding day
People had their thoughts
When celebrating this day
It was the death of Jesus
But he would rise again

Grey Bird

The jet flew overhead
Its underbelly showing grey
Its destination is unknown
The passengers feeling gay
A picture painted on the tail
For a country that is proud
Her heart felt a dread
For something that's ahead
This flight wasn't the one
Twas in the sands of time instead

Guardian Angels

Divine white light shines down
Bathing us in a special glow
It's there every time we look
To stop us feeling low
It can be so powerful
We don't realize why
Our guardians and our angels
Are protecting us just so

Japanese lady

Her heart longed for the land of her birth
Where the blossums fell upon the ground
They bloomed so graceful and beautiful
There is a story to tell
The blossums fall softly from the trees
Their beauty a sea of petals on the ground
She felt grandeur sitting amongst them
It brought the beauty of the lady to life
She glanced demurely around
Hoping no one was watching her
Her hands gently brush the petals
So gentle as not to break them
Her tears in her heart she aches for him
She knows one day he will follow her
They'll hold hands and follow each other
Watching the swallows flying so free

Life

When things hit you in your life
What do you do to heal the strife
Pray for guidance from up above
They will send you heavenly love
All your family and friends are there
Sending their loving thoughts to you
Things are thrown at us to see
If we can cope when we're at sea
Death, destruction, the sick and poor
Is there to show us more and more
So when things hit you in your life
They are there to help heal your strife

Love Unknown

She still dreams every night
She wishes that he were there
Lying quietly beside her
Loving the feelings that they share
The feeling in her heart
Brings her joy and love each time
She wishes they could be together
Her heart nurtured with his love

Moon Eclipse

Rainbow colours reflect the still river
Buildings lit like rainbows on the far shore
A lone black swan swims gracefully around
Coming occasionally to check things out
Seagulls sitting around the waters edge
All lounging about doing nothing at all
The full moon rises burning bright yellow
It's own reflection on the water for sure
The stars twinkle down in the clear sky
Two soft white clouds move gently by
A few voices disturb the peacefulness
Still enjoying the warm evening breeze
The Xmas tree is lit up near the river
Its that time of year for sure

Morning Dew

The birds whistle in the early morn
Waking us up to start the day
Each a different sound from the other
Trying to outdo one another

Flowers blossom in the springtime
The morning dew makes them glow
The trees turn purple in the street
Giving the people a fantastic treat

Trees are lopped around the place
Where will they go to sing their song
I hope they find a place close to me
When the morning dew still glows

Night Dreams

When I was a young child
And supposed to be asleep
I used to peek out the window
Searching the sky so deep

I was beckoned each time
To seek this wondrous sight
The stars and moon so bright
They called to me each night

I look at the face on the moon
And wonder what's on his mind
Then there's Venus and Mars
Twinkling brightly down at me

One morning I awoke older
Knowing that I had seen
The earth and stars below me
I knew where I had been

It wasn't just a dream
To see these joyous sights
Not realising at that time
Angels protect me at night

Night Thoughts

As she lies awake at night
A thought comes to her head
It goes round in circles
Till it drives her round the bend
Her heart and head they fight
Each wanting to win over
The thoughts she has inside
That needs to be aired
The feeling in her heart
Invades her body warmly
Then her head has its say
Not wanting to be ignored
Then she tells them both
Its time to go back to sleep
There she dreams once more
For a love that's in her sleep

Ocean Calling

The ocean calls out her name
Its blue waves roll into shore
The music sounds so sweet
It makes her want to cheer

The sea is soothing to her soul
It helps to make things clear
The sea and sky meet as one
Different shades of green and blue

The water laps around her feet
It cleanses her to the bones
In the distance she see a sail
People feeling free like her

Peace on Earth

People of other nations
Move around the world
To help teach understanding
To everyone on earth
Some feel reluctance
To take them on board
Arguments and demonstrations
Can sometimes be a bore
Patience & understanding
Is needed at this time
When we have achieved this
Peace on earth will reign
Love thy neighbour as your own
This is what its all about
Masses will come together
A peaceful earth will win out

Phone Call

The phone rang'
Her heart sang
The name in her ear
She'd missed all year
Her heart swelled
As they caught up
Memories inside
Came alive
It had been months
She hadn't heard
She didn't care
He was still there
The love she felt
Will never go
Pity he's there
Instead of here

Plane Spirits

Spirits & angels filled the plane
Protecting all of their own
Making sure that we were safe
Bringing a lot of people home
Tourists like me were aboard
Wondering what was ahead
Hoping all would be all right
Knowing this wasn't the end
Over war torn lands we flew
People homeless and alone
The guys below were fighting
With guns in their hands
Some probably didn't stop to think
About our men who were below
We landed safely on the ground
Angels & spirits work was done
They would keep on hanging round
Keeping all safe from all harm

Poems

Poems I like writing
They're there for all to see
The words come out quickly
Messages they can be
The pen can't write fast enough
The ink won't run dry
This is a silly poem
I had to write for thee
Who is thee you say
They are my friends in spirit
Who I need to thank from me
Help me write more poems
I know they come for free

Reality

What is Reality?
Reality is what you make it
Reality is not what you have to own
Reality is your dreams come true
Reality is presence sitting on the beach
Reality is hearing the music of the waves
Reality is what the music is speaking
Reality is the life you are now living
Reality is the life you wish you could live
Reality is up to you to make come true

Reflections of our Souls

Their eyes meet in the mirror
As they drove along
Each reflecting what they feel
A reflection of their souls

Curious questions show
In each others eyes
Their hearts know the answer
That will one day be told

She switches off her mind
To the love she knows
He does the same in front of her
Pulling shades over his eyes

One day they'll tell the other
The way they felt that day
Who knows what will come of it
Their hearts might sing with praise

Restrained Love

People looked at the couple passing by
They saw a love coming from their eyes
Closeness there would always be
An unknown love to other beings
Forbidden love some would say
But felt between them anyway
Brushing skin their hearts stood still
Feelings restrained at their will
Their love is only known to them
Over time it will never wain

Role Reversal

I feel a sense of longing
For a place I used to be
The mother I had years ago
I thought was lost to me
She has come back to share
The life that we have missed
She acts like the mother still
Although our roles reversed

I understand her reasoning
Not wanting to see that place
That caused her lots of sorrow
In a lifetime that sealed her fate
Her instincts have started working
Which she's afraid to show
One day she will realise
It's not so scary to know

Shedding the Past

As I sit and shed the leaves
I have to let go the past
Beginning a new life
Is such a scary thought

My guides and loved ones
Are trying hard to converse
Sometimes I hear them clearly
Sometimes it's hard to say

Where to go from here
I do not know the way
Help me guides and loved ones
So I don't get it wrong again

Someone's Grief

Tears are close to my eyes
My heart feels the pain
Someone is grieving for their loss
Grief will pass, life will start
Their world will be sane again.

Spirit Visit

The room felt as cold as ice
The spirits had came to visit
They all danced around the room
Laughing and chatting as they did it
They had all come to celebrate
She wanted them all to stay
A special thing was going to happen
But what they would not say

Sunday Thoughts

Over the sea the waves do go
Up and down they bob around
Seagulls fly up in the sky
Swooping up and down so low

Sun shines down upon the land
With rain to make things grow
Flowers bloom and look so pretty
Food is harvested to feed the cities

Clouds in the sky form designs
See what you can make of them
Some see Angels, Some see faces
Some see shapes of different sizes

Flames burn bright in candlelight
Dancing round the room
Spirit showing that they're here
Their love is all around us

Music plays to soothe the soul
Messages come from up above
All the living need spirit near
Shielding them with their love

Birds twitter in the trees
Chirping different sounds
Speaking a language in our ear
One we cannot answer

Maidens dancing all around
Like fairies on their feet
Floating up and floating down
They know when they're beat

Car's driving along the road
Disturbance of our peace
Use our feet and exercise
Relaxing us in our sleep

Material things do not matter
Our lives do not need them
Love and peace around the world
Would start another chapter

The Christmas Story

I need a Christmas poem
One that brings us cheer
One I can put out to the world
To let them know you're here
This is a time to celebrate
All that has gone before
The birth of Jesus is the first
Everyone celebrates for sure

As daybreak comes round
The children squeal in delight
To find special treats by the tree
Their eyes are full and bright
It brings their parents glee
Oh what a wonderful day
To see the children play
Not understanding the why
They enjoy the warmth that day

As they grow older they see why
They celebrate throughout the lands
Children tell children the baby Jesus story
About the shepherds and their sheep
And how they came to celebrate

The special event that was a treat
The stars shine brightly above
As the travelers move around
Heading to where the babe was born
To celebrate with the town

Two Hearts

Their hearts felt a passion
That morning in their beds
They both woke with feelings
They knew were hidden there

One heart is scared to think
What may be for it out there
Its life and love and feelings
He knows is hidden there

The other heart has known
The feelings that are there
It came upon her suddenly
When she saw him there

There is hope in her heart
For what she hopes will be
The brain behind his heart
Will see things differently

Unborn Child

The chance was there to know you,
But it was not meant to be.
The mother was unable to birth you,
And look after the other three

If circumstances had been different
You would have had a chance,
But not this time dear loved one,
Although this is not the last dance.

You will come here again,
The time is just not right.
When you do I will know you,
And not let you out of sight.

Understanding

They want to tell their parents
But some don't understand
They have a gene inside of them
That's made them differently
They cannot help the way they are
It's just what's meant to be

Sometimes they may know,
Other times they do not
To come out to ones parents,
Can sometimes cause a shock.
The values of the old school,
Makes it's not the thing to do.

But its time to tell your parents
Let them learn and understand
Some are made of different genes
It's not a secret that need be bad
In time everyone will support you
In time healing will make it right

Wedding Message

The bride and groom are smiling
They're as happy as can be
There'll always be love in their hearts
It's there for all to see

When their children come along
There will be lots of fun and laughter
It will bring them closer together
A happy family they will be

Always talk to one another
Never leave things unsaid
Make the life you share forever
Be the one and only best

Where is the Girl

Where is the girl who hides behind thee
Always hiding to keep from the scenes
The real person she wants to come out
Where is the girl she knows is about
Only a few have seen that girl
Only a few know what a sight
Time has come to shed her skin
To forget the past, to look within
To speak her truth, to share the light
To finally do what she knows is right

White Light

The white light shines bright above
Showing us they're there with love
Never doubt the words you hear
They are there to bring you cheer

Oh white light shining bright
Its not meant to scare or fright
Protect and heal and give us words
Comfort for those who need it most

Who Do They Love

How does she tell the man she loves that the man she loves is the man she loves.
How does he tell the woman he loves that the woman he loves is the woman he loves.
One day the man who loves and the woman who loves tell each other about that love.
Then they spend the rest of their days telling each other how they love one another

Wondering

One wonders what goes on
In minds of people one knows
You think they are friends
But do they really know
The pain they cause at times
You want to write in prose
The real friends you have
You left a long time ago
The world was a different place
A dimension we don't know
We ride a wave like surfing
All through the life we know
Till we reach an age ahead
And know its time to go
Some people are a funny lot
They're scared of what is known
If you teach them to understand
They'll know that place is home

Xmas Sales

The city is alive
Sales everywhere
Adults and kids
Enjoy the atmosphere
Money being spent
Outrageously for some
People will be poor
Before the day is done
Others wander round
Looking at the sights
Not wanting to spend
They can't afford that right

War Poems

These 10 poems are dedicated
to all the soldiers who have lost their lives
fighting in the wars of the 20 & 21st Century

ANZAC Cove 2006

The silence falls over the land
The Diggers are at peace
The poppies have been laid
The lone piper plays his piece

The ghosts of the land have risen
The pilgrims feel a presence there
The emotion each person feels
Has been brought to them all there

The soldiers perished on the shore
As they landed there before
They've come back to the land
In remembrance of before

ANZAC Day 2008

The veterans are all gone
But we still remember them
They fought on tough terrain
For them it was quite a strain
The tears fill my eyes as I watch
The remembrance service each year
I sense I was one from that time
Who had landed over there
I said goodbye at Waterloo
I wouldn't be back again
I went there with my brother
We were together till the end
France wasn't a place I want to see
But need to do before my end
To feel the pain I felt back then
With comrades by my side
The centenary upon us in 7 years
100 years will soon have past
The graves are tended each year
People show they still care

ANZAC Day 2009

The candles burn brightly
Each a spirit from above
Looking down at the people
Remembering their lives with love
Playing the song of Ages Past
The candle flames do their dance
Showing me the spirit world
Is always hanging around
The many men who went to war
Left loved ones home alone
Not knowing with their farewell's
They might never be coming home

ANZAC Day 2010 from France

The spirits of the soldiers gone
Gather round the memorial
It doesn't matter where you stand
To commemorate the past
Sadness, emotion & victory
Has crept inside us all
Tripping round the battlefields
Has been an emotional time
Fallen men are everywhere
All died in another time
Some buried have no names
Some lie where they fell
The pictures in my head
Show fighting that went on
Men digging in the trenches
Men fighting in the fields
Some enjoyed a cup of tea
When there was time out
Men fighting against each other
Because their generals said
All they began to want
Was to be safe in their beds
Xmas they celebrated in 1914

As if they were all friends
Men came from far away
Across the many lands
It started as an adventure
Some wished they never had
The mateship that occurred
Keep the men from going insane
A bond came between them
Which joins the people once again

Atomic Bomb

The sun was shining down
The day the people were made to pay
A bomb fell from the sky
Few were left alive to wonder why

People wandered in a daze
Burned, singed and blown away
The devastation was a sight
Their hearts cried for many nights

People called for water
Their insides were so parched
Each drop they drank was to end
The lives they all had held so dear

There was a man, who helped them all
He did his job till he could do no more
A gentle man who suffered more
60 years later on it still felt raw

Battlefields – Belgium & France 2010

Houses & trees cover the lands
Over tunnels built underground
Bombs lie unexploded
Dug up by farmers ploughs
Cemeteries are all that's left
Of the men who made a stand
Their spirits roam the countryside
Looking down on those around
Seven nations of men took part
All fought to free the lands
The enemy tried to take
What had never been their land

Dedicated to John & the Crew of HMAS Sydney

He was a young man called John
A chef who worked below
He was one who couldn't get out
When their warship was aglow

Feet pounded the teak deck above
Running to who knew where
Men screaming in agony and fright
Their mothers would cry at the sight

Young and old amongst the men
Knowing this was how it would end
The horrific sight around them all
Helping their mates till they cried no more

There was no one around to rescue them
As the ship sank off the coast
Most of them drowned as it went down
Others died from the burns they felt

The men look down from above
Sending to their families all their love
The ship is found where they passed
This will bring closure to all involved

De-Ville Wood – Longeval Cemetery 2010

(South African Memorial)

Bodies lay beneath the ground
The woods an eerie sight
The feeling of peace & serenity
Surrounds us with all its might
Flowers yet to bloom
Will make the scene all white
One day the snow will fall
Turning green into white
One tree is all that's left
From those days gone by
Keeping the secrets of the dead
There is a lot of sadness there
Never have I felt like this
The feelings that I have
They will stay forever in my heart
The tears fell while I was there

To the Soldiers of WW1

The barrel of the guns
Rested in their hands
As they marched forward
Across the bloodied land
War was what they knew
Gunsmoke in their eyes
Horses fell as bullets hit
Bodies covered in flies
Once the war was over
Poppies covered the lands
Red like the blood of soldiers
Remembrance making a stand

Afghan War Zone

The debris scattered the field
The military were dead
There were trying to protect a country
They shouldn't have been there

One man chose this life
From the time he was a child
He knew in his dreams
This would be how it would end

He left three beautiful children
Who would always remember
Their Dad was a mighty hero
They would love till the end

Past Life Poems

Wynnum – Brisbane

As I said goodbye to the bay
I felt a sense of sadness
The shop had closed, an era gone
Along with all the friendships
The wading pool is there for all
It will always be a landmark
Some of the people who live by the bay
Do remember the friendships.
They pushed their prams
Throughout the day
Never forgetting politeness
Something pulls me there each time
And puts the past before me
The feelings are so strong
I know I'll return again
Never will I abandon

Angel in Disguise

Sunlight shined down through the forest
Like a scene from heaven above
A girl was waiting amongst the trees
Barefoot and dressed in rags
She waited as she'd been told to do
For the man who promised her food

Upon his horse he came to her
Her need for him was great
She stood in awe as he reined in
And waited for his gaze
He lifted up his helmet lid
His eyes bore hers with light

He liked what he saw standing there
But could do no more that night
The day would come a long way off
When they'd meet on earth again
She still can't say what's on her mind
Thankful for the food that day

Centuries Old Lovers

Music played in a room not far
They all danced lightly on their feet
A stream trickled over the rocks
Two lovers held hands as they dreamed

They loved each other in that life
They could hear each other's heartbeat
Fate stepped in to change their way
And the plans they would not keep

There was another that he loved
And that was meant to be
They joined together in that life
To fulfill another dream

The lovers met in modern times
Two centuries into the future
They would end up friends again
While he carried out his dreams

Chief Sitting Bull

The chief sits by the campfire
His men are all around
A powwow has been going on
But things are looking dour
Decisions are being made
In their native tongue
Do they stand and fight
Or let the enemy win
The chief says stand and fight
Your men to the very end
Don't let others drag you down
Always rise above them instead
The women watch what's going on
They know there's no way out
Their men will fight by end of day
Widows and slaves they'll be nigh
Chief Sitting Bull this is for you
We knew this could be your end
Thank you for the visit you made
To show me where I must head

Child's Dream

She watched behind the barrel
At the people passing by
She always liked watching
The activity before her eyes
The wharf was a bustling place to be
The sailing ships prepare to leave
Across to the distant lands they went
Where people lived differently
There was a longing in her eyes
She didn't understand why
All she knew was one day
The chance would come her way

A man walks by with bowler hat
He has the same look in his eyes
He knows this child before him
He recognizes it in her eyes
As he reaches out his hand
And promises her a better life
She's knows the time has come
To follow this dark haired man
In her heart she knows just then
That she would cross the sea
To live a life much different
Than what she's ever seen

King Arthur's Mother

Her court stood round watching
Their lady upon the bed
She's been laid out before them
Thoughts swirling in their heads

The pain in her heart had stayed
From a time long ago
When she'd given up her child
To a man who helped him grow

She lived upon a hill
In a castle made of stone
The Dark Ages they were called
But to her it was her home

Water swirled around the base
Merlin waited patiently and quiet
Time would come when it was right
To teach the child what to know

She never traveled very far
This lady who was queen
Her people they protected her
From what was then unseen

She sang and wept through her life
The pain held in her heart
She never saw where he finally lay
But she knew they would never part

Lost Desert Children

Twin girls they were in the desert
Lived there till an early age
A man came along one day
He took them from their ways
Separated from each other
Never meeting till long time ahead
Little toddlers they were when taken
Beautiful happy chubby kids
Sand and dirt they were covered in
And filled with smiles of love
A woman came along who'd miss them
Their taking she tried to delay
The man who was half sleeping
She knew he would cause her pain
Someone come along and woke him
So his deed could be carried that day
The hugging and crying she couldn't stop
Her cherubs taken to the very last stop
Years later on a busy platform
She meet one of her own
All dressed in black and navy
Educated to the bone
She had become a nun
Living in a religious home

The other she meet in the desert
She'd found her way back home
They cried and cried together
Not wanting to leave each alone
The woman child said to stay
They could live together alone
She knew her beautiful babies
Had to live lives of their own

Manor Days'

The picture comes to my mind
A horse drawn carriage driving home
Four people dressed in evening wear
Each enjoying the cool night air
They were staying at the Manor house
Trees secluding it from the road

As they got home and took the stairs
The housekeeper did appear
To make sure her favorite people
Had all arrived safely there
The housekeeper a kindly woman
She thought the daughter her own

As the household lay asleep
A smoulding fire did take hold
Smoke awoke the housekeeper
Who watched the stairway burn
She couldn't get up to rescue them
She could hear the screams of all

One day in another century
A lady turned up for a job
She knew her chance had come

They had an immediate bond
Twas the daughter of the manor house
Their bond formed a lifetime ago

She gave her a job and taught her well
All the things she needed to know
This was her chance to fix the things
She felt deep down in her soul
In future times there will be no debts
They've been paid back threefold

Maypole Dance

We twirled around the maypole
Centuries long before our time
Laughing with gay abandon
Our cheeks and eyes aglow
Till the tears start running down
Telling us it was soon time to go

The clothes we adorned
Showed the era we were in
Long dresses to our feet
Bonnets keeping our hair in
Stockings keeping out the cold
Parents watching from the side

Sisters we were then
Happy and full of pride
Dancing round the maypole
Laughing with such glee
The feeling of abandonment
Bringing warmth to our insides

Sisters or friends we've always been
When we meet up with each other
Friendship, love and tears still there
All through centuries passing by
We will always share our lives
Closeness staying to every end

Loss of a Friend

We knew each other in a life before
Brother or friend I'm not quite sure
We walked along a distant shore
Watching fishing boats bobbing along
We worked together to collect the fish
To take to market to make a dish
In this life we had a friendship
A bond lasting 20 years
I will miss you in this life dear friend
We will meet again in a life ahead

Past War Friendship

They're speak differently
The man and this girl
He helped her to survive
By keeping her at his will
He loved and protected her
In his own special way
The uniform he wore
Is disliked to this day
She wonders why they met
Another lifetime away
Perhaps to repay him back
For the help he gave that time
She feels a bond that's fearless
And knows he feels the same
The age difference is to long
For the past to become today
They've meet for a reason
She wishes she could say
He doesn't want to believe her
But he listens to her ways

Prison Camp

For sixty years there's been sadness
A historic event, I feel I was part of
People annihilated without reason
Soldiers befriended then betrayed them

For some who escaped death
Years of hard work awaited them
Elderly and children got lead away
Thinking they would meet again

Following each other step by step
Not knowing where they headed
They didn't feel scared only a calm
When they saw all the showers

Their angels were waiting there
To take them safely to heaven
After death came the cremation
Others felt fear at smoke arising

Some buried in shallow graves
Fathers and sons had dug that day
No one believed this could happen
Denial of reports they were given

When the war was over
The sad stories came out
Nearly a whole race died
The world wasn't in doubt

Puritans

Puritans they were
Mother and Son
Centuries before
After time had begun

The child rebelled
Didn't like their ways
It happened again
In recent days

Upbringing was strict
But that was a time
People lived a life
They called Divine

The man loved his child
Oh that could be me
He still does in this life
Yes that could be me

For him he still lives
Those Puritan ways
But that is his choice
For me there's no need

Roman Army

They came wearing steel armour
With helmets to protect their heads
They marched across the land
Taking over whenever they can

They marched along the leafy lanes
Scaring everyone in sight
The children watched behind the hedges
Not sure what would happen that night

Where to go, what to do
The people did not know
They took their fate in their hands
And stood up to their foe

The Roman Army kept on going
Following orders that were gave
From coast to coast they marched
Known as heroes till this day

Sailing Ship

The ship sailed the ocean waves
The boy scrubbed the decks all day
A couple stood by the rail
Talking of where their future lay
The boy dreamed of a better life
But drowned by end of day

Slave Friend

He came from an island
This man I've meet before
We meet many lives ago
Upon a distant shore

Our lifetimes have changed
They will change again
Until our Karma's
Bring us together again

The time we knew each other
Bought a feeling to my heart
I thought I'd lost forever
Left behind with cotton balls

The day we said goodbye,
Our feelings were the same
Fate keeps us close but far apart
To meet again a lifetime away

Smugglers

Water splashed against the city walls
The Thames night an eerie sight
Smugglers creeping round back alleys
Into the caverns needing light

Lanterns help to shine the way'
Hoping underground is found
Down the steps into the earth
They do not make a sound

Dressed in black they blend in well
Rowers waiting to make light
They find the goods they need to move
They will make a profit on that night

The brother with him he knew quite well
They have lots of secrets they don't tell
They meet each life as centuries pass
Their bond lasting forever

Titanic

The iceberg loomed before them
The sky was clear for all to see
The ship went down to the bottom
Fifteen hundred souls lost dreams

The crew of this beautiful lady
Tried to save them all from peril
But their efforts were in vain
Only a few could escape free

No one could come to their rescue
Help was more than a day away
When it arrived it was to late
A few souls survived that day

The wreck lies at the bottom
Along with artefacts and bones
For the divers who are curious
All wanting to make their claim

People try to re-enact the story
Millions made from others plight
Leave the ship to rest in peace
Survivor's memories of the night

Channelled Messages

Visitation and Channelled Message from Jesus

The light was so bright
It completely filled my mind
Then Jesus stood before me
Magnificent in his sight
He said things would be alright
All we have to do is pray
He had me kneel before him
Then next I felt his touch
I felt the white light through me
My soul was filling with his love
"Don't worry about other people
He said they all had to learn
Their issues aren't your issues
It's their time to learn
We stumble in our lives
But this just makes us strong"
"Help me Help Jesus
Is all you have to say
I will stand before you
And guide you along the way
Some know what their plan is
Some have to find their way"

"It's not hard when you listen
Just ask and I will say
I send my love to you all
And watch down on you all day
My spirit came back to show you
That this is another life
On a different dimension
But still very close to self"
"There maybe a touch on your shoulder
Or a gentle breathe in the air
When you feel this is around you
You know I'm always there"
I said to him send healing
With your healing hands
His reply to me was white light
He sent healingt from where he stands
Thank you thank you Jesus
The privilege is so great
Pray come again and help me
With messages that relate

2nd Visitation and Channelled message from Jesus

"I am the Son of God, I am here to help you all
The world has been suffering, through famine and war
You need to stop the wars; you are all one people,
People need to help one another,
This I have told people when I was on earth before"

The white light gets brighter, as I listen to his words,

"You need to spread my word,
Tell people about the light, it's there inside you all"

Q. Jesus will people believe what I tell?
A. They will when they read the words,
 They will feel a warmth inside,
 My words will comfort them,

Once again I knelt before him,
And felt the warmth of his hand on my head,
Go forth and tell the world he said,
"I am here to listen to anyone who calls"
We will talk again he said,
He will help me speak his word.

Channelled message after Doreen Virtue's Angel Intuitive Seminar Australia 2010

Jesus came through a beam of light
His brilliance shone oh so bright
"Go forth tell the world of Angel Realms
Tell the people what you've learned
Tell them all about the light
Tell them all about what you felt
People walk in different forms
Each with a plan for their highest good
The wise amongst us bring us cheer
Angels everywhere show they care
People will listen when you speak
All you need is to release the fear
Cut the cords you feel are there
Angels will help you – ask tonight!"

Message from Arch Angel Metatron

You need to be doing the work
It helps the people to grow
We are proud of what u did today
The spirit world applauds you
We are watching you grow
I am Metatron I am your guide
We will send our healing light
Healing can be done anywhere
Not just the healing room

Event Poems

Aussie Outback

Life has changed much in the outback
Gone are the horses, camel and pack
Planes and trains now take their place
Travelling takes hours instead of days

The soil is red and full of dust
Never wear white it will look like rust
The rains do come and the rivers flow
Wildflowers appear giving a special glow

It's a special breed who plant the seeds
Up in the early hours to avoid the heat
Some ride on horseback for long days
Moving the stock across the way

The animals can survive the heat
They find shelter to help them sleep
The children love to help and play
They share their learning by airwaves

The mothers are there to lend an ear
Cook and clean, they do their share
The neighbors' always lend a hand
No one will ever deny this land

Australia Day

They came to celebrate on the shore
The day Australia came to the fore
The colours in the sky were bright
It made the people cry with delight

Police patrolled to calm the crowds
A job well done, despite the hours
The youngsters were all well behaved
They gave us pride back on this day

The fireworks went off with such a bang
It caused the peoples breath to hang
The people dispersed without a murmur
To celebrate another year further

Boxing Day Tsunami

They were a happy nation
The people who lived by the sea
The tourist's come, the tourists go
They spend plenty of money
Which helped feed and clothe
A wave of water strikes their shores
Leaving more people dead
Then they have known before
It destroys their homes
The young and old
Millions left homeless
Looking for one another
Hundreds of thousands died
This was a terrible plight
The people of the world unite
Send relief to this terrible sight
The scene will never fade
The scars will always stay.
People of the world wont forget
Boxing Day Tsunami that came

Camden Town

Fire rages in Camden Town
People swarm onto the streets
Flames shoot high in the air
Sparks flying all around
People are sad to watch it go
Frightened by the orange lights
Markets, restaurants, and nightclubs
Sadly burning to the ground
Fireman there to put flames out
Policemen and women they help out
Not a lot left to show what's been
A famous part of Camden Town

China Earthquake

The rubble falls around
Buildings lie on the ground
Children buried underneath
Many dead beyond belief
Parents standby watching
Hope showing in their eyes
Rescuers try their best
To bring up those who are alive
Vehicles and buildings crushed
People running from the rush
Thousands died once again
Why it's happened we wonder
There has to always be a reason
Just like there is always a season

Days Gone By

The people worked hard
From morn to night
Enduring the same each day
They churned the butter
They sewed the clothes
They washed the dishes
They mended the hoes
They sowed the fields
They made the bread
Teaching their children
For their lives ahead

The men chopped wood
They built the sheds
They tended the animals
Which made them grow
That in the end
Helped feed and clothe
They taught their sons
To be strong and brave
As their time would come
To lead the way

The hardship of the days gone by
Was felt by one and all
They were of strong character
And had strength of will
No one could imagine
How they survived those days
But this was normal life to them
Never did they complain

Dedicated to the Victorian Bush Fire Victims

Fire burned all around them
They saw their death approaching
Their lives flashed before them
Like a movie in slow motion

Children who hadn't been here long
Knew they were on their way home
Their parents felt the pain inside
As they watched their children go

As each adult followed their child
They saw a light before them
It was their children reaching out
To take them by the hand

They led them to a heavenly place
Where white light would heal them
It would take away the scars
Of the people who died in cars

Como Cinema

The old theatre still stands
The old movies are now new
The people in the audience
Are dressed to avoid the flu
Hats and coats of another era
Heaters to keep them warm
It all looks aged and old
The patterns on the walls
Seating from another era
Has stood the test of time
People stood as music played
God Save Our Gracious Queen

Haiti Earthquake

Devastation hits again
The people of Haiti not to blame
Earthquakes rip apart their land
There's barely any room to stand
Buildings tumble all around
People buried – not a sound
Survivors frantically look around
Family and friends couldn't be found
Food and aid finally gets through
To feed the starving there were a few
Miracles happen – voices heard
Calling for help from beneath the earth
Children and elderly survived the nights
Despite the cold and the fright
People worked with bare hands
To remove the debris fallen down
One of the poorest nations on earth
Have felt this destruction before
Never to the scale that hit this time
They will recover and build again
A better standard the world will see
Their grief and loss will eventually leave

Headhunters

Headhunters from time long gone
Their Spirit still lingers on
Attached to spears that they held
Oh what a story they could tell
The spears look evil in their stance
People's heads had been attached
You can feel the pain at the door
Blood spots stain forever more
You still feel the energy that's around
Masks and spears they were found
I felt like I had crossed a void
Where time had once stood still
Ancient artefacts are what they are
Bought from afar into our world
The people of our modern world
Don't realise what once occurred

New Orleans Drowns

The world looked on
As disaster struck
An old city drowned
Modern homes broke

Factories burned down
That couldn't be put out
A tornado called Katrina
Wrecked havoc all round

A million were homeless
Ten thousand were dead
People were starving
They were living in dread

They started out looting
For what they could get
But they soon came realize
They needed food instead

Help was long coming
From a country so big
Finally troops arrived
With choppers full of food

Orders had been given
No tolerance allowed
Anyone caught stealing
Would fall to the ground

Holidaymakers lost and scared
Where could they look for help
They watched a modern city
Turn into a third world

They banded together
To keep themselves safe
Till they finally were given help
One of their own got them out

Perth Bush Fires

The bush fires have been a sad sight
Giving the people a terrible fright
The city is surrounded with ash and smoke
A lot of people are starting to choke

Homes and human lives were spared
But there was a person who didn't care
He destroyed the wildlife and their homes
Leaving the vegetation to regrow

The city was in a haze for days
The fireman deserve a lot of praise
They fought the fires for hours and hours
Wondering when they would sleep again

Samoan Tsunami

People of the pacific unite
Devastation what a sight
People drowning, bodies lost
Their lives washed away
Their world was lost
People remained to rebuild
Time will take life to return
All the angels who can help
Send the Samoans' love and light

Space Flight

They take off safely into the sky
The lovely bird finally flies
The spirits from a previous flight
Accompany them firing into the night

They circle the globe then off they go
Into the atmosphere we don't know
There's work to do out there for others
To make things safer for their brothers

The work is done, its time to go
They will meet again another time
Back to earth which is the plan
Safe and sound to the cheers on land

Sumatra Earthquake

Sumatran people have felt the pain
Earthquakes happened once again
Bodies buried under cars and rubble
No food or water for the starving
Dogs and rescuers looking all night
Hoping to find the people alive
It feels like life has come to an end
They wonder what's around the bend
Please Angel realms and all who can help
Send love and healing to them tonight

Train Wreckage

The mist lies low
An eerie sight
Hiding the wreckage
Throughout the night
It protects the souls
Waiting to take flight
The bells still flash
The ringing still sounds
The wreckage is strewn
Along the ground
People's belongings
Hiding the facts
The healing will start
When all is cleared
Memories will be shared
By the living and dead.

Victorian Bushfires

Country towns in Victoria
Burnt quickly to the ground
People from these towns
All devastated by the loss
Whole families gone to rest
While others counted the cost
The country rallied around
Donating whatever was found
One hopes the fires go out
And no more lives are lost

Experience Poems

Britain Experiences

I left the shores of Britain
Two and half hours later in the day
I had spent 5 weeks time there
And had a ball every day

From John O'Groats to Lands End
I saw most things on the way
The people all spoke different accents
I listened hard to hear them say

The history that surrounded me
I felt inside my bones
The castles, lochs and churches
I never felt alone

The buildings of my ancestors
I was fascinated to see
They all seemed to jump out
And say hey look at me

Culloden & Glencoe were places
I saw the fighting with my sight
The crofts that lay in ruins
What happened to their lives

With the majestic mountains
I saw prehistoric in my mind
People had lived there long ago
Surviving anyway they knew how

The air was clean in the highlands
The sun out on most days
But down the south its inhabitants
Breathe smog in their airways

The ruins of Tintaginal
What an awesome sight
Standing on a rocky outcrop
Feeling on top of the world

Deep down in my inside me
I felt a world of centuries ago
Telling me to come back again
And stay longer next time round

The Cornish land was calling me
Just like Scotland had before
The coastline was very rugged
Green and Blue met at the shore

The country roads are narrow
Cars and buses pulling over
Drivers waving to each other
Showing courtesy on the way

The ruins of old mines go by
People's living now well past
The graveyards show the evidence
Others immigrated to advance

The Cornish are a friendly bunch
They segregate from the rest
Like Kiwis and Aussies in the world
They are proud and think they're best

Cambridge and Oxford you must see
Rain or shine the uni's gleam
The architecture blows you away
You want to sit and look all day

Stonehenge and Avesbury are a feat
Stones upon stones and some on their own
Villages in circles and some with sheep
Don't stand with the Leyline at your feet

The little villages throughout the land
All have something to give them a stand
Thatched roofs and quaint pubs
Smiles on faces for all to see

London is an exciting place
It takes time to get to know it
Double Decker's & Cathedrals dominate
At 1 pm you always know it

The colours are so vibrant
A mixture of the world is there
From Notting Hill to Camden Town
Piccadilly Circus to who knows where

The underground oh what a sight
Tracks and trains go left and right
A maze of tracks in the bowels of the earth
An engineering feat they made to serve

Trains rattle along at a very fast pace
How ever will they stop at the station
Then you know the driver braked
We stop dead at the right platform

Above ground trains are hard to use
If you're a tourist and have a suitcase
Just puff and pant like everyone else
When you get to the top you will know it.

So ends my trip to my ancestral lands
The money spent well worth it
The land will call me back again
When I have time to make it

Group Outing

The group was an interesting blend
People of all different trends
Quiet & serene, friendly & happy
Shaky & nervous, two of them snappy
One was the outsider standing her own
Waiting to see if her cover was blown
Cover you say, oh what a day
Nice as can be, everyone was free.

First Passenger Train to Mandurah

The train came along the track
Everyone held their breaths
Waiting in quiet anticipation
To board the train going south
Finally it crawls silently in
Carriages filling to the brim
Most of us tried to squeeze in
Some were left standing about
The train was free to Mandurah
Everyone came from all about
Young, old, and infirmed
Enjoying what it was about
Perth to Mandurah had happened
The train speed down the track
Dad and Grandad whispered
Telling me they were there
Time ticked by as we all held on
The driver making us laugh
Every stop we came to
No one wanted to get out
People waited on the platforms
Disappointment on their faces

They had to wait another train
And hope their turn came round.
We finally arrive in Mandurah
Smiles and cheers all around

Incense Burns Out

As the incense burnt down
The smoke fades away
I said goodbye with tears
To the Dad I love so dear
He said to me in return
Don't cry I am always here
I am always at your side
Watching everything you do
I see the final spark go out
And feel him then depart
The air that had been so thick
Has now gone quite clear

Keukonhof Tulip Farm

Flowers bloom its tulip time
Never again would I see so many
Every colour you could imagine
Perfuming the air smelling pretty
Noise & chatter break the silence
Spoiling a day where it's all serene
Languages different from one another
Chattering away engrossed in each other
Blooms sway gently in the breeze
Flags fly softly near the trees
People click away with cameras
Savouring a moment for others to see
We all have to return to the city
Pictures in our heads forever to keep

Leaving Japan

As the tears roll over my heart,
The plum blossoms start to bloom.
The people of this nation,
Have left a mark upon my soul.
All of you whom I have met,
Have been so very kind.
I came from a distant shore,
It was time to meet you all.
Thank you for all the friendships,
I'll treasure them all my life.
We have formed a bond between us,
That will always feel so strong.
Do not despair when I'm not here,
I will be back again some day.
My ears hear the language,
My tongue cannot speak.
But this hasn't stopped,
The communication we keep.
I will remember this beautiful land,
Feelings will pull me here again
Arigato Gozimasu

My Ghost My Sister

She can't help the way she is
But understands more we know
As she danced in her own way
Her mother danced beside her
I saw my sis in a ghostly form
I wanted to watch all day
To see this figure dancing there
With her daughter it blew me away
I felt comforted in the knowledge
As I turned and walked away
I am sad that I wasn't able to say
I wouldn't be back for many a day
Telling this beautiful woman
Would have upset her ways
Sister keep protecting her
All the years she's here

Orbs of Spirits

The orbs of spirits were all around
They followed me from town to town
If I was down or insecure
Photo's I took to be so sure
I felt them there inside my head
They were with me even though dead
They kept me safe as I travelled around
On the trains and in the air
I just listened and they were there
People also from ages past
Of era's before everyone was fast
Painters, artists, royalty and more
Soldiers who had died in the war
I saw you all around the graves
In trenches, tunnels, all terrains
Never let there be a doubt
You're not forgotten you're always about
Thank you guys for being there
Giving me hints when things weren't clear
Dad, Sis, Nan and many more
I got your hints and even more
Rest in Peace my brigade of friends
I look forward to contact to the end

Sleepy Town of Reefton

Reefton is a wee wee town
Where not much can be heard
Listen hard in the early morn
You may hear the wee wee birds

Surrounded by mountains all around
The fog and smoke lays low
Then sun peaks through the clouds
And everything is aglow.

The streetlights are but a few
Making the town look bright
Some buildings from an era past
Looking grand to my sight

The bearded miner's campfire
Bought a smell from long past
The friendliness is the same
As the years of long ago

The miners work for gold and coal
They bring money from the ground
One day when riches are gone
There'll still be a sleepy town

Scottish Feelings

My heart filled with tears
The day I said goodbye
The clans have surrounded me
On this rugged island shore

The Gunn's & McDonalds,
McAlister's & Williamsons,
Fraser's, and many more
All have a strong history
That goes back years before.

At Culloden I saw the fighting
Men dying before my very eyes
The same happened at Glencoe
The men dying another time

My heart felt the pain
Both times I saw the past
The tears rolled down my cheeks
The sadness not a surprise

As I walked the Glasgow streets
Ancestors pointed buildings out
They knew in their lives
One was planned them self

It was good to have there
Protecting me all the time
Knowing they were there
This was their song

I saw the clans all gathered
Playing songs of farewell
They are saying come again
They'll be there just the same

I want to stay here longer,
Experiencing the feelings again
The communication I was having
That some don't understand

Suburban Sunday Train

Sitting on the train
All heading somewhere
People sitting opposite
Trying not to stare
Hiding behind sunglasses
Not letting their thoughts bare
Boy & girl sit cuddling
Like it's their last goodbye
Grandparents going visiting
It's just another train ride
They stare around the train
They've done it all before

Scenery changes many times
Going suburb to suburb
Houses become different
Old suburbs and new
Trees line the tracks
Graffiti adds to the view
If you're really lucky
The sea pops through the trees
Mobile phones all working
Clogging up the airwaves

Conductors check tickets
Dilemma is what one feels
The ticket hides itself
Without the kitchen sink
Face reddens embarrassed
Everyone around stares
The conductor wants to fine
The ticket pops up last minute
He looks and gets off the train
Checking tickets on another line

The Seal

He was swimming round & round
When I went underground
He's happy in his environment
Looking out and all around

When he saw me standing there
A great display did he put on
Each lap he did was on his back
Till he reached in front of me

Then he turned himself over
Took a breath and came at me
He stared me straight in the eye
Each time he came around

He was sending me a message
Even though he made no sound
I wanted to touch this seal
And feel his pulse beat within

He was reaching inside my mind
It was like he wanted to grin
Spirit was telling me while I stood
My friend was doing just for me

This special display of cheekiness
That bought us all such glee
Spirit talked to my seal friend
And told him I was there

So we shared a moment
It might never happen again
I didn't want to leave my friend
But this sight I had to share

Other people wanted pictures
They would show to all that night
My seal friend would treat them all
The memories they would keep

The Weatherman

The weatherman had pride of place
Upon the window sill
It sat there for many years
And would have sat there still
The little lady and little man
Used to pop in and out
To tell us what the weather would be
And not leave us in any doubt.

When the Dad did the dishes
He always checked them out
He sometimes used to flick them
Just to watch them pop in and out
The daughter grew attached to it
And wanted it one day for herself
So she could stand and do the dishes
And always check them out

One day the mother decided to sell
The weather house on the sill
Someone else was doing the dishes
And always checking them out
Tears flowed down the daughter's cheeks

She cried inside for a week
She wanted back the weatherman
So she could look at it herself

It had been in her life since she was a tot
It was considerably old
Now the weather lady and man
Have been so sadly sold
One day she would like it back
To show kids of her own
Then they could wash the dishes
And always check them out

Visitors

The lights on the hillside
Were shining so bright
A strange sight this must be
Flying Objects could they be

Being discreet as they must be
No one is supposed to see
I wondered if this was true
Until I heard people saw it too

Wynnum Foreshore

The sea glitters in the sun
The sky is blue above
The wadding pool still being rebuilt
The children will soon have fun

The islands sparkle in the distance
Looking remote but not far off
People fishing off the jetty
Enjoying the peace and quiet

The splashes of water hit me
As I sit on the rocky steps
The wind blows gently round me
Creeping into my very soul

The buildings are being made modern
New replacing old along the shore
One day there will be nothing left
To show what was before

Xmas Long Ago

The highlights in my life
Don't come to mind too often
I sometimes want to cry
For things that are forgotten

I picture in my mind
A special Xmas day
Grandees came to visit
Goodies came our way

It was the time they spoilt us
I loved those happy days
Fun and laughter we shared
Which lasted all the day

It showed a family life
We didn't have so often
Those times are gone alas
But they won't be forgotten

Famous People

Chilean Miners Rescue

The big day came
The men were freed
Their mates had worked
To fulfill their needs
The men buried below
Had shown a strength
Beating the odds
Against natures best
The nation wept
As the men appeared
The church bell tolled
The first time in years.
The men were buried
For sixty plus eight days
They supported each other
Till there rescue ended
One man didn't survive
He came up from below
His soul departing earlier
Leaving everyone above

Free Man

He came to this country
To live as a free man
The years spent in the camp
Made him strong for this land

He made lots of friends
Spokesman for them all
He gave them loads of help
Till they found their way along

One man had other reasons
He let their friendship grow
He gained the trust of everyone
Of all those he'd come to know

He travelled miles across the land
For the task which he'd chosen
To take the life of this kindly man
Who wouldn't know what happened

At the time of his death
All he felt was the pain
They struggled for a moment
Then the darkness came

He knew his life was over
Things would never be the same
The Angels came to get him
Taking him back to his land

Dark Knight

Dressed in his purple suit
With his Oscar in his hand
He stands guarding the theatre
Watching everyone in awe

The timbers give a feeling
Of the darkness of the night
The bright lights give a feeling
That the entire world is bright

Standing on the stage
They will feel you about
Your acting will live on
Inspiring young and old

Hearing peoples comments
You know they are so proud
It's been a place of pilgrimage
Your spirit will always live on

Lasseter's Reef

The desert is gold
Barren and sand
The aborigines stand
Spears in their hands
Knowing the land
White man before them
Looking for the gold
He finds the reef
But he dies alone
It's Lasseter's Reef
The aborigines know
But won't tell a soul
The dreamtime is theirs
No one else is to know

Dedicated to Michael Jackson

You loved to dance your heart out
Thrilling people with your moves
Your songs poured from your lips
Thrilling people with your words
Your voice was soft & quiet
Sounding feminine to our ears
The music that you sang
Stayed with us through your years
You were a beautiful person
No matter what was portrayed
You'll stay in the hearts of many
Your music part of our history

Dedicated to Vincent Van Gogh

A writer that I am
An artist that he was
Van Gogh left his mark
Everyone can now see

His passing in 1890
Unnoticed in those days
Another time would be
In the 20th Century

In the middle of a field
Landscape at Twilight
A name it would make
It would bring delight

Sitting in the sunshine
At the top of his house
Looking out over rooftops
He let this thoughts come out

Crows in the Wheat fields
Was what came to his mind
It become a famous painting
The last of its kind

Family Poems

Betty

As I lay in bed a sleeping
In the wee hours of the morn
I felt a warmth surround me
That kept me awake till dawn
The news in the morning
Bought a sorrow to my heart
You had journeyed into god's hands
And joined your family who had past
You were a lovely lady
A lady who had so many friends
A mother who was loved so dear
A sister who always cared
An aunty and a grandmother
You're loved by one and all
You've been through much yourself
But you were always there
You will hold a special place
In everyone's heart
Even those who can't be there

Joined her Spirit Family 2005

Bessie

I was given a family environment,
They treated me like their own.
Some devastated by the separation,
Most have never disowned.
Brothers and sisters you'll always be,
With support that's very rare.
I know deep down if I need you,
I can call and you'll still be there.

The years were a long struggle,
For the mother who bore you all.
She instilled values and love,
As each of you were born.
She was loved by everyone,
My love no less than yours.
Her strength and will was strong,
Throughout her seventy-five years.

Having had a bush upbringing,
She knew that this was the way.
She was very proud of her children,
And all their offspring have achieved.
Some veered off the tracks awhile,
Her love for them never changed.
She enjoyed travelling around,
Spending time with one and all.

If I ask you for your help,
I feel your presence when I call.
One day we'll all meet again Bessie,
Everyone will get to see.
We are part of the same soul family,
I can feel you looking down on me.
You were the best mother in law,
One could ever hope there'd be.

Joined her Spirit Family 1986

Boy Next Door

Special people come into our lives
To teach us things we need to know
You are one of those special people
That I have always known
You are always there strong and free
You never have a bad thing to say

We all know and love you
In so many different ways
You attached yourself to our hearts
When you were the little boy next door
You are the loved son, brother and friend
You are special in so many ways

Trips into the unknown fascinate you
Experiencing all life has to give
Spreading your wings as time goes by
Learning more on your flight
Making friends with everyone
Never an enemy in sight

Busy Bakery

Andy Pandy makes pudding & pie
To feed the people who pass by
His fame will spread far & wide
They all flock in as time goes by
The taste he makes will linger on
Stay in the memory of those past by

The staff is ruled by a firm hand
If things go wrong Y makes a stand
Everyone knows to get it right
Else they know it's out of sight
The busy baker is their dream
To pull this off will be the cream

Family Pictures

Looking at all the photos
I see before my eyes
I wish all these people
Were still in our lives
I know you are in spirit
And with us all the time
Not being able to talk to you
Brings tears to my eyes
You all look so young
Your lives still ahead
The joining of the families
The challenges yet to face
As a result of you all
We came into this world
To meet all the challenges
You had faced them all

Jim

The call has come for you to go
To your family on the other side
You have left a saddened family
Your time has come we know
You worked the soil for dawn to dusk
Farming you loved to do
You had some trials in your life
But your life was joyous to
The suffering you had to endure
No longer causes you pain.
The angels will look after you
Every step along the way
I want to say from all of us
Even though you've gone away
We will love you just the same
Your name will always stay

Joined his Spirit Family 2006

Maori Princess – Channeled From Nana

The Missionary's came
To teach about the light
They spread the word
To make things right
Our tribes lived in pas
Feeding off the lands

Flax skirts we made
They were so bright
We traded them off
When ships pass by
For trinkets and guns
And other things

We tended gardens
Where veggies grew
To feed our men
To help them grow
To make them strong
To wars they'd go

A white man came
He took my hand
He led me south
To the white snow
Laying on the ground'
Where I had to stay
I was his princess
Its how the story goes

Man on the Hill

He's hammered nails since he was a kid
This snowy haired man on the hill
He's sawed and nailed all his life
The houses are standing still
Around the country he used to travel
Working hard each time at his trade
Houses popped up everywhere
With his joinery filling him with pride

Mum

She left us to return home
Family & friends waited there
We will all meet again
When we too return there
She fulfilled the plan she made
Before she came to this earth
To teach us things we need to know
They were lessons we had to learn
She now looks down from above
And watches all we do
The hopes and dreams we all have
It's up to us to make come true

Joined her Spirit Family 2006

My American friend

I feel a poem coming on
About a friend in "USA"
By coincidence we meet online
And get along just fine
He has a sense of humour
Only few can comprehend
He always has an answer
Which makes me laugh no end
He doesn't believe in what I say
Try as I might to make it so
We understand each other's ways
And debate them to the end
We were aboard the same war ship
One day back in seventy-three
He was on his way to Asia
We under training we had to do
That was the closest our paths crossed
Until the Internet came along
We formed a great friendship
Based on that day years ago
One day he got very sick
He thought that he had gone
But he came back to say
He wasn't wanted this time round

I sent healing to him every night
Till I knew he was well
And now I have to start again
As his problems seem to swell
I feel I knew him in the past
He would scoff at that idea
And tell me that I was nuts
And to get out of here
But I just laugh cause one day
He'll see what I've been saying
I will come back to haunt him
He will know me in his dreams

Nan

You were always needed
You were the greatest Nan
You understood how it was
Through our growing years
The times I lived with you
Were the happiest of my life
You sung and played the accordion
Those tunes still come to my head
It takes me back to those days
I felt warm and loved inside
I see you standing at the bench
Cooking lunch and having a beer
The chats we used to have
The memories that we shared
Will stay with me forever
I know you are still here
We had a special relationship
I thought I'd never have
Looking down from spirit world
I still feel your guiding hand
Thank you Nan for being there
You are still such a dear

Joined her Spirit Family 1990

New Born Child

A boy who was born the seventh day
A boy who was determined to stay
A boy who was sent to this earth
A boy who will do well in life
A boy who will do no wrong
A boy who will make his way
A boy who will keep his family strong
A boy who will be loved by one and all

Over the Air Waves

There is a lady who's out there
She plays her music on the air
The people love what they hear
It brings them all a lot of cheer
They dance and jig around the room
When they hear the 1 o'clock boom
She plays the music for young and old
While her father watches down with love
Keep playing Maggie you're such a dear
For the happiness you bring to those out there

Poppy Brian

There he lay broken hearted
Thinking he would like to pee
He looked down and saw the bag
Wondered when he would be free

As he lays back on his bed
His arm resting above his head
He starts to become quite dramatic
But we all knew this was automatic

He really is a loving man
He fights his sickness bravely
Each time things get inside of him
He finds the strength to fight them

I will never forget this dear man
He's a sturdy rock around us
Come what may, I'd like to say
Please keep him here forever

Joined his Spirit Family 2007

A picture of young and old
You were seventy-five
I was a few weeks old
There was wiseness about you
It was there for all to see
You knew all the families' trials
But never judging what you see
You and Nan were wise
And never said a thing
You loved us all no matter what
From your house by the sea
You came to me this morning
I knew that it was you
Surrounding me in your love
I want to say Thank you

Joined his Spirit Family in 1974

Sís

I loved you sis with all my heart
I never wanted you to go
It tore me up to much to bear
I couldn't accept it was so
The pain I felt at that time
Buried itself deep inside
I had to bring it to the fore
To let the guilt go with pride
It wasn't my fault that you left
I had to release my thoughts
And know this was your destiny
To be in the spirit world again

Joined her Spirit Family 1991

Steam Train – For Dad

The steam train chugs down the track
Smoke billowing from its funnel
The fireman in the engine cab
Looks ahead towards the tunnel
Darkness looms as they chug along
It looks an eerie sight
A smile comes upon his face
He loves the feeling of the night
The firebox open, the coals aglow
He shovels more the faster they go
Through the hills till they meet the snow
The plough on the engine is ready to go
He lived in a hut beside the track
His wife and child beside him
His baby listened to the sounds
The trains going clickety clack
The fireman knew when the whistle blew
His day's work had begun
The oil cup sits upon the shelf
It has a pride of place
A souvenir that he was given
From the last steam train on the track

Passed to his Spirit Family 1989

Talented Child

She was a long awaited child,
This lovely daughter of mine.
From when she arrived on earth
She was the apple of my eye.
When she was three,
She could write the same as me.
When she was five,
She could bring music alive.
When she was seven,
She wrote stories made in heaven.
When she was only nine,
She played "A song for Guy".
The applause was so loud,
It made me very proud.
When she was eleven,
She gave a welcome speech,
To a well known author,
Leaving everyone in awe of her
When she was sixteen,
She won a scholarship to Japan,
To stay a whole year,
It seemed too much to bear.
She learnt a new culture,

For that we are grateful.
Four years into university,
She's learning all she can.
One day she will finish,
All her dreams before her.